Mastering Cold Emailing

A Practical Guide for Businesses

By Stefan Florin

Table of Contents

Chapter 1: Introduction – Cold Emailing Still Works

Chapter 2: The Legal Landscape of Cold Emailing

Chapter 3: Building a Cold Email Strategy

Chapter 4: Writing Winning Cold Emails

Chapter 5: The Psychology of Cold Emailing

Chapter 6: Finding the Right Prospects

Chapter 7: Timing and Frequency

Chapter 8: Avoiding Spam Filters

Chapter 9: Automating Cold Emails

Chapter 10: Case Studies and Success Stories

Chapter 11: Measuring Success

Chapter 12: Scaling Your Cold Email Outreach

Chapter 13: Common Mistakes and How to Avoid Them

Bonus 1: Cold Email Subject Line Cheat Sheet

Bonus 2: Overcoming Common Cold Email Objections

Bonus Resource: Cold Email Wizard

Chapter 1: Introduction – Cold Emailing Still Works

Cold emailing often gets misunderstood. Some people swear it doesn't work anymore, while others think it's nothing more than spam. But let me be clear: cold emailing still works—if you do it right. Over the years, I've seen it open doors, generate leads, and grow businesses. It's one of the most direct and effective ways to connect with potential clients or customers. This book is going to show you exactly how to master it.

Overview

Why does cold emailing still matter in today's marketing world? Because it puts you right in front of your audience. When you send a cold email, you're not hoping that someone scrolls past your ad or clicks on your post. Instead, you're landing directly in their inbox—a space they check regularly. And while not every email will hit the mark, when you do it right, cold emailing can generate the kind of targeted, qualified leads that are hard to come by elsewhere.

What most people don't realize is that cold emailing isn't just about mass sending a generic pitch and hoping for the best. It's about doing the work—researching your audience, crafting a clear and compelling message, and sending it in a way that feels personalized. The key isn't volume; it's relevance.

Why Cold Emailing Remains a Powerful Tool

Cold emailing lets you take control. You're not relying on algorithms to show your content, nor are you paying for expensive ad placements. You're creating an opportunity, one email at a time, to speak directly to someone who could benefit from what you're offering. Whether you're in sales, marketing, or business development, cold emails are a practical way to introduce yourself to new contacts, establish relationships, and get a foot in the door.

Think about it. Everyone has an email account. People check their emails multiple times a day. And even though inboxes are often crowded, well-crafted cold emails stand out — because they're personal, relevant, and clear. If you can catch the recipient's attention within the first few seconds, you're already ahead of the game. It's all about creating that moment of curiosity, getting them to open the email, and sparking enough interest that they want to respond.

My Story: How I Got Here

Let me introduce myself. My name is Stefan Florin, and I've been an internet marketer for about 8 years. Over these years, I've worked with businesses and entrepreneurs to help them improve their marketing efforts. From SEO to ad campaigns, I've seen a lot of marketing tactics come and go. But one thing that has always been a constant in my work is cold emailing.

Not only have I helped others build successful email campaigns, but I've also been an affiliate marketer myself for nearly as long. This means I've lived and breathed the challenges of trying to get someone's attention through an email. I've written countless emails, sales scripts, ad copy, landing pages, and website content. So, when I tell you that cold emailing works, it's not just theory. I've used it to grow businesses, including my own.

This book is my way of passing along everything I've learned — both the successes and the failures — so that you can use cold email marketing to your advantage. I've made the mistakes, and now I'm here to make sure you don't have to. The strategies I'll share are tried, tested, and proven to work.

Common Misconceptions About Cold Emailing

Before we dive into the nuts and bolts, let's clear up some common misconceptions about cold emailing:

- **"Cold emailing is just spam."** No, it's not. Spam is unsolicited, irrelevant, and often deceptive. Cold emailing, when done correctly, is a targeted and thoughtful outreach to someone who might benefit from what you offer. The difference is in the approach.

- **"Nobody reads cold emails."** That's simply not true. If people aren't reading your cold emails, it's probably because the emails aren't relevant to them. If you make the message clear, concise, and valuable, people will read and respond.

- **"Cold emailing is outdated."** Not at all. In fact, cold emailing has evolved. What's outdated are the spammy tactics of the past. Today's cold email strategies focus on relevance, personalization, and delivering value. When done right, cold emailing is as effective as ever.

Chapter 2: The Legal Landscape of Cold Emailing

Before we dive into crafting cold emails, let's get something straight: cold emailing is legal — as long as you follow the rules. It's not just about protecting yourself from penalties but about maintaining a professional, trustworthy reputation. The legal framework around cold emailing isn't as complicated as it seems, but it's critical to understand and respect it. In this chapter, I'll walk you through the basics so you can confidently send emails without worrying about getting flagged or fined.

CAN-SPAM Act

In the United States, cold emailing is governed by the **CAN-SPAM Act** (Controlling the Assault of Non-Solicited Pornography And Marketing Act). This law is designed to protect consumers from misleading or unwanted emails. While it doesn't make cold emailing illegal, it does lay out several requirements you need to meet. Failing to comply with CAN-SPAM can result in hefty fines so it's worth understanding the key points:

- **Identify yourself clearly.** Your "From," "To," and "Reply-To" fields must accurately represent who you are. No pretending to be someone else. If you're emailing on behalf of your business, use your business name. If it's personal outreach, use your own name.

- **Be honest with your subject lines.** Don't try to trick people into opening your email. Your subject line must accurately reflect the content of the message. For example, if you're offering a discount, make that clear. Don't promise something in the subject line that you don't deliver in the email.

- **Include a valid postal address.** Every cold email must include a physical address where the recipient can contact you. This could be your business address, a P.O. box, or even a registered commercial mail service. This is a straightforward requirement, but it's easy to overlook—especially if you're sending bulk emails.

- **Provide a clear way to opt out.** You must give recipients a simple, clear way to unsubscribe from future emails. This is usually done with a link at the bottom of your email, but it can also be a note that says, "Reply with 'unsubscribe' if you no longer wish to receive emails from us."

- **Honor opt-out requests quickly.** Once someone opts out, you must remove them from your email list within 10 business days. After that, you cannot contact them again unless they explicitly opt back in. No more follow-up emails, no more offers. Just move on.

GDPR: For Your European Contacts

If you're emailing people in Europe, you'll also need to be aware of the **General Data Protection Regulation (GDPR)**. GDPR is much stricter than CAN-SPAM, and the penalties for violations can be severe, ranging from fines to bans on sending emails within the EU. Here are the key aspects:

- **Consent is required.** The biggest difference between GDPR and CAN-SPAM is consent. Under GDPR, you need explicit consent from the recipient before you can send them marketing emails. This means you must have some kind of prior relationship with the person, or they must have opted in to receive emails from you.

- **Legitimate interest.** In some cases, you can email without consent if you can prove a "legitimate interest." This could apply if the recipient is a business contact, a potential client, or someone who has shown interest in your product or service. However, this is a gray area, and you need to tread carefully. If the recipient complains, you could still be held liable.

- **Right to be forgotten.** GDPR gives people the right to have their personal data completely erased from your systems. If someone requests that you delete their information, you must comply. This means not only removing them from your email lists but also erasing any personal data you've stored, like names or email addresses.

- **Transparency.** You need to be upfront about how you're using personal data. This means explaining why you're emailing them, how you got their information, and what you plan to do with it. Make this clear in your privacy policy, which should be linked in your email footer.

Other Regulatory Bodies and Considerations

It's important to note that email marketing isn't just regulated by the laws I've mentioned. Agencies like the **Federal Trade Commission (FTC)** in the United States and other regulatory bodies around the world are responsible for enforcing these rules. The FTC in particular takes consumer privacy seriously and investigates complaints about companies that violate email marketing laws.

Beyond the FTC, other countries have their own specific laws related to cold emailing. For example:

- **Canada's Anti-Spam Legislation (CASL):** Canada has one of the strictest anti-spam laws. Under CASL, you must have either express or implied consent from the recipient before sending a commercial email. The penalties for violating CASL can be up to $10 million CAD.

- **Australia's Spam Act:** Similar to CASL, Australia's law requires you to have consent before sending commercial emails. You must also include a clear unsubscribe option and your contact details in every email.

- **UK Data Protection Act:** Though the UK follows GDPR, it also has its own data protection laws that apply to email marketing. Post-Brexit, this may evolve further, so it's important to stay updated if you're targeting UK audiences.

Stay Safe: Honor Opt-Out Requests

One of the easiest ways to stay compliant is by honoring opt-out requests. If someone tells you they don't want to receive any more emails, stop emailing them. No exceptions. This applies to both CAN-SPAM and GDPR, but it's also just good business practice. If someone's not interested, move on to the next potential client. It's far better to focus on engaged leads than to risk damaging your reputation—or worse, getting fined.

The Role of Email Service Providers

Many email service providers (ESPs) have strict anti-spam policies as well. Services like MailChimp, Constant Contact, and others will shut down your account if they suspect you're violating spam laws. These providers have systems in place to ensure compliance, such as mandatory unsubscribe links and tracking email engagement. However, they're not a free pass—you're still responsible for knowing and following the law.

The Bottom Line

Cold emailing is perfectly legal in most parts of the world, as long as you follow the rules. Laws like the CAN-SPAM Act, GDPR, and CASL are in place to protect consumers, and as long as you respect those boundaries, you're in the clear. The core principles are simple: be honest, provide value, and give people the option to opt out. By sticking to these guidelines, you'll not only avoid legal trouble but also build trust and credibility with your audience.

Chapter 3: Building a Cold Email Strategy

The success of any cold email campaign starts with a solid strategy. Sending emails without a clear plan is like throwing darts in the dark—you might hit the target occasionally, but you're mostly wasting time and energy. In this chapter, I'm going to walk you through the process of building a cold email strategy that works. A well-thought-out strategy makes the difference between a campaign that gets ignored and one that generates responses, leads, and conversions.

Identifying Your Target Audience

Let's start with the most important question: Who are you emailing? Cold emailing works best when you target a specific audience. Focus on people who are most likely to benefit from what you offer. The clearer your audience definition, the higher your success rate.

- **Get specific with your audience.** Don't just target "business owners" or "marketers." Instead, narrow it down: Are you targeting SaaS founders? Local plumbers? Marketing directors at eCommerce brands? The more specific you get, the more you can tailor your message.

- **Use data to inform your targeting.** Don't rely on guesses. Look at industry data, analyze your current customers, or use tools to gather information about potential prospects. Consider factors like industry, company size, geography, and pain points to build a well-defined list.

Segmenting Your List

Once you've identified your target audience, it's time to break that group down into smaller segments. Why? Because not all of your prospects will respond to the same message in the same way. Segmenting your audience lets you send targeted emails that speak directly to specific subgroups, ensuring more relevance and personalization.

- **Job titles and roles.** If you're emailing both marketing managers and CEOs, they're going to have different concerns. Tailor your messaging accordingly.

- **Industry specifics.** A cold email sent to a tech startup founder should look different from one sent to a local contractor. Each industry has its own language, challenges, and needs—make sure you're speaking directly to those.

- **Behavior-based segmentation.** If you have prior interaction with a segment—maybe they've opened a previous email or visited your website—you can create a more personalized follow-up email based on those actions.

Crafting Compelling Value Propositions

Now that you know who you're emailing, the next step is to craft your **value proposition**—the reason your recipient should care about your email. This is where many people go wrong. They focus on what they want (a sale, a meeting, etc.) instead of focusing on what the recipient needs. Your value proposition should answer the question: **"What's in it for them?"**

Here's how to build a strong value proposition:

- **Focus on benefits, not features.** It's easy to list the features of your product or service, but what matters most to your recipient is the outcome. How will what you're offering make their life easier or solve a problem they have?

- **Be specific.** Generic promises like "We'll help you grow your business" are too vague to be compelling. Instead, say something like, "We've helped companies like yours increase their inbound leads by 20% in three months."

- **Align with their pain points.** Address their pain points directly and demonstrate how your solution solves their problems.

Personalization: Balancing Relevance and Scalability

Balance personalization with scalability by using recipient names and company details in your emails, and reference specific aspects of their business when possible. You don't need to rewrite every email from scratch, but you should avoid sending cookie-cutter templates.

- **Use their name and company.** At the very least, your email should address the recipient by name and reference their company. Tools like mail merge or cold email software can make this easy to automate at scale.

- **Mention specific details.** If you know something about their business, mention it. For example, if you saw that they recently launched a new product or service, acknowledge that in your email. This shows that you've done your homework and aren't just sending a mass email.

- **Keep it relevant to their industry.** Personalization also means crafting messages that make sense for their industry or role. If you're emailing someone in the construction industry, talk about problems related to construction. Avoid sending irrelevant or generic messages.

Writing the Cold Email: Short, Clear, and Actionable

When it comes to cold emails, **brevity is key**. People are busy and don't have time to sift through long emails. Keep your emails short and to the point. Introduce yourself briefly, provide immediate value, and focus on a single, clear call to action. This forces you to focus on clarity and purpose, ensuring that every word counts.

Here's how to structure a winning cold email:

1. **Subject line**: Make it short, direct, and intriguing. Consider using a curiosity-driven subject line, like "Where do you source [specific product] from?" or a direct approach like "Helping [their business] increase leads by 20%."

2. **Opening line**: Get straight to the point. Briefly introduce yourself and immediately reference why you're reaching out. Example: "Hi [Name], I noticed that [their company] recently [specific observation] and thought I could help with [specific solution]."

3. **Value proposition**: Be concise and focus on the two-sentence pitch. Highlight how you can solve a problem or achieve a goal, and tie it directly to the recipient's needs. Example: "We've helped businesses like yours reduce churn by 15% using a simple strategy. Do you have 10 minutes this week to discuss how we could do the same for you?"

4. **Call to action**: Keep it simple and low-pressure. Instead of asking for a large commitment, offer a quick chat. Example:

"Do you have 10 minutes this week for a brief chat to explore how we can help?"

5. **Signature**: Keep it professional, concise, and free of clutter.
   Example:
   Best regards,
   [Your Name] | [Your Company] | [Your phone number]

Remember, the goal is to start a conversation, not close the deal. Keep your emails short and engaging, and avoid overwhelming the recipient with too much information upfront.

Testing and Iterating Your Emails

Even the best cold email strategy isn't perfect right away. You need to **test and iterate** based on the results you're getting. Don't assume that your first attempt will be your best.

- **A/B test your subject lines.** Subject lines are crucial for open rates. Try testing different variations to see what works best. For example, test a question versus a statement, or personalization versus a generic approach.

- **Experiment with your value proposition.** Sometimes what you think is a strong value proposition doesn't resonate with your audience. Test different value propositions to see what resonates — one might emphasize time savings, while another focuses on cost reduction. Measure which approach gets the most responses.

- **Analyze the data.** Keep track of your open rates, reply rates, and conversion rates. If you're not getting the results you expect, make changes and test again. Pay attention to patterns in what's working and what isn't.

Follow-Up Strategy

The fortune is in the follow-up. One email usually isn't enough to get a response. Most people won't reply to the first email, and that's normal. Your follow-up emails should be just as thoughtful as your first message.

- **Don't spam them.** Space out your follow-ups over a few days or even weeks. Two or three follow-ups are usually sufficient.

- **Add value in each follow-up.** In each follow-up, offer something new and valuable—such as a case study, an article, or additional information that demonstrates how you can help—rather than simply asking, "Did you see my last email?"

- **Stay polite and professional.** Cold emailing is about building relationships, not pushing too hard. Keep your tone friendly and respectful, and don't pressure them to respond.

Conclusion: The Foundation for Success

Building a cold email strategy is about more than just sending emails—it's about sending the **right emails** to the **right people** at the **right time**. By focusing on your audience, crafting compelling value propositions, and constantly refining your approach, you set yourself up for success. This chapter lays the foundation for the rest of the book, where we'll dive deeper into the specifics of writing, sending, and automating cold emails that get results.

Chapter 4: Writing Winning Cold Emails

To get results with cold emailing, you need to focus on clarity, relevance, and providing value. The goal is to craft an email that grabs attention and encourages action. Forget about trying to be clever or using flashy language. Instead, write emails that speak directly to the recipient's needs and provide a clear reason for them to engage with you. In this chapter, we'll break down the elements of a successful cold email and how to structure it for maximum effectiveness.

The Anatomy of an Effective Cold Email

A cold email is a carefully crafted message, not something you send out and hope for the best. Each part of the email serves a purpose in capturing attention and leading the recipient toward the action you want them to take. Here's what each element should achieve:

1. **Subject line**: The door to your email.

2. **Opening line**: Captures their interest and gives them a reason to keep reading.

3. **Value proposition**: Explains the purpose of your email and why it matters to them.

4. **Call to action (CTA)**: Tells them what you want them to do next.

5. **Signature**: Ends professionally with your details.

Let's dive into each element in detail.

Subject Lines That Grab Attention

The subject line is the first thing your recipient sees. Its job is simple: get them to open the email. Sometimes, the simplest approach works best. For instance, using a two-pronged approach can work wonders, particularly in competitive niches. Start with a vague but intriguing question that's still relevant to the recipient's business, sparking curiosity. For example, "Where do you source your hot sauce from?" This opens up a dialogue instead of directly pitching, which can feel too aggressive in the initial interaction. Once the recipient responds, you can dive into the brief pitch that solves a specific problem.

- **Be specific, but succinct**: If you're not using a curiosity-driven approach, ensure your subject line hints at the content of your email. For example, instead of being vague with terms like "Quick follow-up," try something like, "Helping [their company] increase leads by 20%" or "Can we help you with [specific challenge]?"

- **Use curiosity strategically**: If using curiosity in your subject line, make sure it aligns with the email's value. Misleading subject lines will backfire if they don't tie into a meaningful pitch in the body of the email.

Examples of strong subject lines:

- "Where do you source [specific product] from?"
- "Can we help you solve [specific problem]?"

Opening Line: Hook Them Immediately

Your opening line sets the tone for the rest of the email. You've got just a few seconds to make them decide whether they'll keep reading or hit delete. Get straight to the point and avoid fluff.

- **Personalize right away.** Start with something that's relevant to them, like their business, their role, or a recent event. Example: "I noticed that [their company] recently expanded into [new market], and I wanted to share a strategy that could help drive more local leads."

- **Avoid unnecessary introductions.** Don't waste valuable space with long intros about yourself or your company. Keep it brief and focus on how you can help them. Example: "I help businesses like yours increase customer acquisition through targeted email campaigns."

- **Get to the value quickly.** You don't have time to build up to the value proposition—get there fast. By the second sentence, the reader should have a clear idea of why you're emailing them and what's in it for them.

Examples of effective opening lines:

- "Hi [Name], I noticed your company is growing fast, and I think we can help you reach more customers with a targeted ad strategy."

- "Hey [Name], I've worked with a few companies like yours, and we've seen great results with a simple change in how they approach lead generation."

Crafting a Clear and Compelling Value Proposition

Your value proposition is the heart of your cold email, and when targeting business owners or decision-makers, clarity is key. The **two-sentence pitch** approach is highly effective for this audience because it respects their time while quickly demonstrating value. For instance:

- **Example of a two-sentence pitch**: "We specialize in helping eCommerce businesses increase conversions by optimizing product pages and checkout processes. Do you have 10 minutes this week for a quick chat?"

The key to success here is being concise. Aim for no more than two sentences in your pitch, and always end with a clear call to action. Business owners appreciate directness, especially when they are pressed for time.

- **Be specific and concise**: Instead of a long-winded description, focus on the result you can deliver. For instance, "We helped [Company X] reduce customer churn by 15% using a simple change in their marketing process. I'd love to see if we can achieve the same for you."

- **Highlight the benefit, not the feature**: Even when you're brief, ensure the benefit to the recipient is clear. Business owners are more interested in how you can solve a pain point than in the technicalities of your solution.

- **Use social proof if possible.** If you've worked with similar companies or have strong case studies, mention them. Example: "We recently helped [Company X] increase their inbound leads by 30% in just three months using this strategy."

Examples of value propositions:

- "We've developed a lead generation system that's helped similar companies generate 50+ new leads per month, without increasing their ad spend."
- "Our solution can help [Company] reduce customer churn by 15% in the next six months by improving engagement with existing clients."

Call to Action: Clear, Simple, and Direct

The call to action (CTA) is one of the most critical parts of your cold email. You've caught their attention, provided value, and now you need to guide them on what to do next. The CTA should be clear, simple, and low-pressure.

1. **Make it easy for them to say yes.** Depending on the relationship with the recipient, you can either assume interest or ask for confirmation. If you're emailing warmer leads, assume they are interested by asking something like, "When do you have time for a call this week?" For colder leads, you might want to ask for confirmation instead, such as "Are you available for a quick chat on Thursday?" Both approaches can encourage quicker responses, but the key is to match the tone to the recipient's level of engagement.

2. **Don't overwhelm them with too many choices.** Stick to one clear CTA per email. If you ask for too many things, like a meeting, a reply, and checking out a link, it becomes overwhelming and reduces the likelihood of a response.

Examples of effective CTAs:

- Assuming interest: "When do you have 10 minutes for a quick call this week?"

- Asking for confirmation: "Would you like me to send over a case study on how we helped similar companies?"

The Signature: End Professionally

Your **signature** is more than just a formality. It should provide the recipient with your contact details and any relevant information they might need to follow up. Keep it professional and straightforward.

- **Include key contact details.** Make sure to include your name, company name, phone number, and email address. This shows you're legitimate and easy to reach.
- **Avoid clutter.** Don't overload your signature with too much information like logos, social media links, or multiple phone numbers. Keep it clean and concise.

Example of a clean signature:

Best regards,

[Your Name]

Founder & Email Marketing Specialist

[Your Company]

[Phone number] | [Email address]

Examples of Different Email Structures Based on Target Industries

The structure of your cold email may vary slightly depending on who you're targeting. Below are a few examples of how to adapt your message:

For B2B SaaS companies:

- **Subject**: "How [Company] can reduce churn with our SaaS tool"
- **Opening**: "Hi [Name], I noticed your company has been growing quickly, and I wanted to share how our software can help you retain more customers."
- **Value Proposition**: "Our tool has reduced churn by 20% for similar SaaS companies, saving them thousands in lost revenue."
- **CTA**: "Can we schedule a quick call this week to see if it could work for you?"

For Local Businesses:

- **Subject**: "Helping [Company Name] attract more local customers"
- **Opening**: "Hi [Name], I see that your business is well-established in [City], and I wanted to share a way we've helped similar businesses grow their local presence."
- **Value Proposition**: "We specialize in helping local businesses get more foot traffic through targeted social media and SEO campaigns."
- **CTA**: "Do you have time for a short call on Thursday to discuss?"

Conclusion: Keep It Short and Simple

At the end of the day, the most effective cold emails are those that are clear, relevant, and direct. Keep your emails short—ideally no more than 25-30 words. This forces you to focus on getting to the point quickly, which maximizes the chances of engagement. A concise email is much more likely to generate a response than one overloaded with details. Remember, your goal with cold emailing isn't to close the deal immediately—it's to start a conversation. If you can grab their attention and show them how you can help, you've done the hardest part. Everything else follows from there.

Chapter 5: The Psychology of Cold Emailing

Understanding human psychology is crucial when writing cold emails. The key isn't just in the words you choose but in how those words influence the recipient's thoughts and actions. People don't make decisions in a vacuum—they are guided by emotions, logic, and social cues. In this chapter, we'll explore the psychological factors that can make your cold emails more effective and help you connect with your audience on a deeper level.

Building Trust with Cold Prospects

When you send a cold email, you're essentially a stranger entering someone's inbox. This means your first challenge is to build trust quickly. Without trust, your email won't be taken seriously, no matter how great your offer is.

- **Use a professional tone.** Sounding professional doesn't mean sounding stiff. Use a tone that feels conversational but respectful. Be mindful of being too casual, especially if you're reaching out to executives or decision-makers in more formal industries.

- **Keep it human.** People prefer engaging with a person, not a generic corporate entity. Personalization helps build trust— use their name, reference their business, or mention a specific detail to show you've done your research.

- **Leverage social proof.** Mentioning other businesses or people who have benefitted from your product or service helps build credibility. If you can reference a well-known company or case study, it immediately boosts your trustworthiness. For example, "We recently helped [Company] increase their sales by 25% using our method."

The Power of Simplicity and Clarity

One of the biggest mistakes in cold emailing is trying to be too clever or overwhelming the recipient with too much information. People respond best to simple, clear messages.

- **Avoid jargon or buzzwords** that can confuse or alienate the reader. Stick to simple, clear language that's easy for anyone to understand.

- **Get to the point fast** — your opening lines should immediately explain why you're reaching out and how you can help. Don't make the reader dig through long paragraphs to understand your value.

- **Make it easy to act.** Your call to action should be obvious and simple. Don't leave them guessing about the next step. Whether it's scheduling a call or downloading a resource, make it clear what you want them to do and how they can do it with minimal effort.

Understanding the Buyer's Journey

Every recipient is at a different stage in their buying journey. Some may be completely unaware of your product or service, while others might be in the research phase or even ready to make a decision. The effectiveness of your cold email depends on how well you align your message with where they are in that journey.

- **Awareness stage:** At this stage, your prospect may not even realize they have a problem that you can solve. Your goal here is to educate them and introduce them to the issue. For example, "Are you finding it hard to convert leads into customers? We've helped similar businesses solve this problem."

- **Consideration stage:** Here, the prospect is aware of the problem and is looking for solutions. Your email should focus on demonstrating why your product or service is the best option. Highlight specific benefits and features that set you apart from competitors.

- **Decision stage:** When the recipient is close to making a decision, your cold email needs to focus on closing the deal. This is where case studies, testimonials, and strong calls to action come into play. Show them why acting now will benefit them immediately.

The Principle of Reciprocity

People are wired to return favors. If you offer something of value upfront, your prospect may feel inclined to respond. This psychological principle, called **reciprocity**, is a powerful tool in cold emailing.

- **Offer value upfront** — such as free advice, a resource, or an invitation to a webinar. For example, 'I'd love to send over a guide on improving email marketing — let me know if you're interested.'"

- **Keep it genuine.** Don't make your offer sound like a gimmick or sales tactic. Be sincere in your willingness to help. If your email feels like it's pushing too hard for a response, it can have the opposite effect.

The Fear of Missing Out (FOMO)

People don't like missing out on opportunities, and leveraging this can drive action. However, you need to use FOMO carefully and avoid making your offer feel like a cheap sales tactic.

- **Create urgency.** For example, you can add urgency by mentioning limited availability: "We're offering 10 free consultations this month—let me know if you're interested in claiming one."

- **Highlight exclusivity.** People value things that feel exclusive or limited. Phrasing like, "This offer is available to a small group of businesses like yours," can make the recipient feel special and motivated to act.

Social Proof: Harnessing the Bandwagon Effect

People tend to follow the actions of others, especially when they feel uncertain. Social proof—showing that others have benefited from what you offer—taps into this psychological tendency.

- **Use testimonials or case studies.** When you reference other businesses that have seen success with your solution, you reduce the risk for the prospect. For example, "Companies like [Company A] and [Company B] have seen a 30% increase in sales after working with us."

- **Highlight the number of clients or industries served.** Stating that you've worked with 100+ businesses in their industry can reassure them that you know what you're doing.

The Power of Asking Questions

Asking a question in your cold email can be a great way to start a conversation and engage your recipient. A well-placed question encourages the prospect to think and respond, which increases your chances of getting a reply.

- **Ask open-ended questions.** Instead of asking yes/no questions, ask questions that invite more detailed responses. For example, "How are you currently handling lead generation?" or "What's your biggest challenge when it comes to scaling your business?"

- **Keep it relevant.** Your question should be closely related to their business or industry. A question that feels random or irrelevant will only make them tune out. Show that you understand their business and that you're genuinely curious about their needs.

The Psychology of Loss Aversion

People are more motivated to avoid losing something they have than to gain something new. This concept is known as **loss aversion**, and it can be a powerful motivator in cold emails.

- **Frame your solution as a way to avoid losses.** Instead of focusing only on potential gains, emphasize how your product or service helps them avoid a problem or setback. For example, "By not optimizing your email campaigns, you could be missing out on 20% more leads every month."

- **Highlight missed opportunities.** Remind prospects of missed opportunities if they don't act. For instance, "Without a solid lead generation strategy, you risk falling behind competitors."

The Gender of the Sender and Perception

Research shows that the perceived gender of the sender can impact how cold emails are received. For example, emails sent by individuals with gender-neutral names or those perceived as women may receive higher open and response rates in certain industries. While this effect varies depending on the recipient's own biases or industry norms, it's worth considering how the sender's name might influence response rates. If appropriate, A/B test using different sender names to determine what works best for your audience.

Conclusion: Aligning Psychology with Strategy

The psychology behind cold emailing is about understanding what motivates people to act. By tapping into concepts like trust, reciprocity, social proof, and loss aversion, you can create emails that not only capture attention but also drive action. Each email you send is an opportunity to connect with a potential customer in a meaningful way. By aligning your messaging with these psychological principles, you're setting yourself up for higher response rates and better results.

Chapter 6: Finding the Right Prospects

One of the biggest mistakes in cold emailing is sending your message to the wrong people. Even the most perfectly crafted email won't get results if it's sent to someone who doesn't care or isn't the right fit. The more precise you are in selecting your audience, the more likely you'll generate responses and, eventually, conversions. In this chapter, we'll walk through the process of identifying and finding the right prospects for your cold email campaigns.

The Importance of Targeting

Finding the right prospects requires a thoughtful approach. The better you define your audience and qualify your leads, the more effective your cold email campaigns will be.

- **Know your audience.** Before you even think about sending an email, you need to be crystal clear on who your ideal customer is. Are they CEOs of small businesses? Marketing directors at tech startups? The more specific you can get, the easier it will be to find them and craft messages that resonate.

- **Focus on quality over quantity.** It's tempting to think that the more people you email, the higher your chances of success. But a smaller, well-targeted list of high-quality prospects will often outperform a large, untargeted one. Not only will your engagement be higher, but you'll also avoid wasting time on people who were never going to respond in the first place.

Where to Find Your Prospects

Once you know who your ideal customer is, the next step is to figure out where to find them. There are several tools and strategies you can use to locate your target audience, depending on your industry and goals.

- **LinkedIn:**
  LinkedIn is one of the most powerful platforms for B2B lead generation. With its advanced search features, you can filter prospects based on job title, industry, company size, and even geographic location. This makes it an ideal place to find decision-makers in almost any sector.

- **Company Websites:**
  Many businesses list key decision-makers on their websites, often under the "About Us" or "Team" sections. You can gather names and job titles here, then use email finder tools to track down their contact details.

- **Industry Forums and Groups:**
  For niche markets, industry-specific forums, Slack groups, or Facebook groups can be gold mines for finding prospects. People who participate in these communities are often vocal about their needs and challenges, giving you valuable insight into how you can approach them.

- **Email Databases and Lead Generation Tools:**
  Tools like **Hunter.io**, **Snov.io**, **Apollo**, and **ZoomInfo** can help you find the email addresses of prospects based on their company's domain. These tools offer robust features like bulk email searches and data enrichment, helping you build lists quickly and efficiently.

Pro tip: Always verify the emails you collect using tools like **NeverBounce** or **ZeroBounce** to ensure that the addresses are valid.

Sending emails to invalid addresses can damage your sender reputation and affect your deliverability.

Qualifying Your Prospects

Just because you've found a list of potential contacts doesn't mean they're all great prospects. Qualifying your prospects ensures that the people you're reaching out to are a good fit for what you're offering. This step helps you avoid wasting time and increases the likelihood of success.

- **Demographic fit.** Does this person match the profile of your target customer? Consider factors like their job title, company size, and industry. For example, if you're offering a SaaS product for small businesses, a prospect from a Fortune 500 company may not be the right fit.

- **Pain points.** Are they likely to have the problems that your product or service solves? For instance, if you specialize in helping companies with digital marketing, target prospects that are actively investing in online marketing but may need help scaling their efforts.

- **Decision-making authority.** Are they the person who has the power to make or influence purchasing decisions? You don't always need to reach the CEO, but you should focus on people who can either make decisions or are directly involved in the buying process.

- **Budget considerations.** Can they afford what you're offering? There's no point in pursuing leads who don't have the budget for your services. Doing a bit of research into the financial health of the company or the typical budget for their industry can help.

Segmenting Your Prospect List

Once you've built a list of qualified prospects, it's important to segment them. Not every prospect should get the same email. By segmenting your list, you can tailor your messaging to different groups, increasing the relevance and effectiveness of your emails.

- **By industry.** Different industries have different pain points and needs. For example, an email to a tech startup should focus on speed and scalability, while an email to a local retail business might focus on increasing foot traffic.

- **By company size.** The size of the company can significantly affect the way you pitch your product or service. Larger companies may need enterprise-level solutions, while smaller businesses may be more interested in affordability and ease of use.

- **By role.** Tailor your messaging based on the recipient's role in the company. A CEO might be more interested in big-picture results, while a marketing director may be focused on specific strategies and KPIs.

Researching Your Prospects

A little research can go a long way in helping you craft personalized emails that stand out. By gathering some basic information about your prospect and their company, you can make your emails feel more relevant and increase your chances of getting a response.

- **Check their LinkedIn profile.** Look for recent posts, articles, or comments. These can give you insight into what's currently on their mind and help you frame your message accordingly. For example, if they've recently posted about a challenge their company is facing, you can mention it in your email and offer a solution.

- **Review company news.** Take a few minutes to scan their company's website or Google News for recent updates. Have they launched a new product? Expanded into new markets? Mentioning this in your email shows that you're paying attention and that your outreach is tailored specifically to them.

- **Look at competitors.** If you've helped similar companies in their industry, mentioning this can provide instant credibility. For example, "We've worked with [Competitor] and helped them increase their ROI by 20% in six months. I think we could achieve similar results for you."

Tools for Finding and Managing Prospects

To streamline your efforts, here are some popular tools that can help you not only find prospects but also manage them efficiently:

- **LinkedIn Sales Navigator:** Offers advanced search filters and lead recommendations to help you find the right people based on their roles, industries, and company sizes.

- **Hunter.io:** Helps find email addresses associated with specific company domains. You can bulk search for contacts or find them individually based on a prospect's name and company.

- **Clearbit:** Allows you to gather detailed information about a prospect or company, such as revenue, number of employees, and industry, which helps in better targeting.

- **Apollo.io:** Provides a rich database of verified email addresses and contact information, allowing you to search prospects by title, industry, location, and more.

- **HubSpot CRM:** An excellent tool for managing your prospects once you've found them. It allows you to track email interactions, store contact information, and manage follow-ups efficiently.

Conclusion: Precision in Prospecting

Finding the right prospects is about being intentional. The more precisely you define your audience and qualify your leads, the more effective your cold email campaigns will be. Tools like LinkedIn, email databases, and prospect research platforms can make the process easier, but they are only as good as your targeting and research efforts. Take the time to segment and personalize your outreach, and you'll significantly increase your chances of connecting with the right people and getting the results you want.

Chapter 7: Timing and Frequency

In cold emailing, when you send your emails is just as important as what you say. Timing can make or break your campaign, while frequency determines whether you come across as persistent or annoying. Understanding the best times to send emails and how often to follow up can significantly increase your chances of getting a response.

Why Timing Matters

Timing is critical because it determines whether your email lands in a crowded inbox during peak hours or in a quieter period when your recipient is more likely to read it. Sending an email at the wrong time can result in it getting lost in the noise, but getting the timing right can increase the chances of your message being opened, read, and responded to.

- **Inbox overload**: While most people check their emails multiple times a day, they often receive a flood of messages, especially during working hours. If your email arrives when the recipient is overwhelmed, it might be overlooked.

- **Decision-making windows**: Depending on the recipient's role and industry, there are specific times when they are more open to making decisions or scheduling calls. Timing your email to align with these windows can help increase your chances of success.

Best Times to Send Cold Emails

While there is no universal answer, research and experience suggest that certain times generally yield better results. The key is to consider the recipient's work habits and industry, and to experiment with unconventional timing.

- **Weekdays work best, but weekends can surprise**: While professionals often check their emails regularly from Monday to Friday, sending emails over the weekend can work well in some industries. Small business owners, for example, may check emails outside regular hours, and emails sent just before or after a business's open hours may catch them with fewer distractions.

- **Personalized sending windows**: Tailor your send times to a business's specific operating hours. For example, sending emails two hours before a business opens or after it closes can increase the likelihood that decision-makers will notice your message.

- **Early morning or late afternoon**: Emails sent early (7 a.m. to 9 a.m.) or late in the afternoon (4 p.m. to 6 p.m.) tend to perform well, as people often check their inboxes first thing in the morning or toward the end of the workday.

- **Adjust for time zones**: If you're reaching out to prospects in different time zones, be sure to adjust your email timings accordingly. Tools like email schedulers can automate this process, ensuring your emails land at the right time for each recipient.

Testing Your Timing

General rules about timing are helpful, but every audience is different. What works for one group might not work for another, so testing is essential.

- **A/B testing**: Try sending emails at different times, including unconventional hours like weekends or late nights, to see what works best for your audience. For instance, emails sent outside typical 9-to-5 hours could yield better open rates in certain industries.

- **Review open and response rates**: Track open and response rates for different times. Over time, you'll notice patterns that help you identify the most effective times to reach your prospects. Also, don't overlook general addresses like info@; these are often forwarded to the owner's inbox.

The Importance of Frequency

Getting the timing right is crucial, but knowing how often to follow up is just as important. Follow-up emails are key to getting results, but sending too many can become irritating.

How Often to Follow Up

Balancing persistence with respect for your prospect's time is essential. Here are some guidelines for follow-up frequency:

- **2-3 follow-up emails**: For most campaigns, two or three follow-up emails are sufficient. Send your first follow-up 3-5 days after the initial email. If there's still no response, follow up again after a week.

- **Avoid daily follow-ups**: Bombarding someone with daily emails will damage your credibility and could result in your emails being marked as spam. Give prospects enough time—typically 3-7 days—to respond between follow-ups.

- **Space them out**: Each follow-up email should be spaced out by a few days or a week. This gives the recipient time to consider your offer without feeling pressured.

What to Say in Follow-Up Emails

The content of your follow-ups matters as much as their frequency. Each email should add value rather than simply reminding the recipient that you're still waiting for a reply.

- **Reference the original email**: Start by reminding the recipient why you're reaching out. For example, "I wanted to follow up on my previous email about helping [Company] with [specific offer]..."

- **Add new information**: Offer something new in each follow-up. Share a case study, provide useful advice, or mention a recent development that could benefit them.

- **Keep it brief**: Follow-up emails should be concise. You've already introduced yourself, so focus on nudging them toward a response by asking a direct question or suggesting a time for a quick call.

Example of a follow-up email:

Hi [Name],

I wanted to follow up on my email from last week about helping [Company] streamline its lead generation process. We recently worked with [Similar Company] and helped them increase their lead conversion rate by 20% in just three months.

Do you have a few minutes this week for a quick call to discuss how we can achieve similar results for [Company]?

Best regards,
[Your Name]

When to Stop Following Up

Knowing when to stop following up is as important as knowing when to follow up. After a certain number of emails, it's better to move on than risk annoying the recipient.

- **Three or four attempts**: After three or four emails, it's time to stop. If they haven't responded by then, they're either not interested or too busy to engage. Continuing to send emails might hurt your reputation.

- **Leave the door open**: Your final follow-up should be polite and leave room for future communication. For example, "I understand you're busy, so I'll stop reaching out for now. If you're ever interested in discussing [offer], feel free to contact me."

Example of a final follow-up:

Hi [Name],

I know your schedule is likely packed, so I'll stop following up after this message. However, if you're ever interested in discussing how we can help [Company] with [specific problem], please don't hesitate to reach out.

Best regards,
[Your Name]

Automating Timing and Frequency

Managing timing and frequency manually can be time-consuming, which is where email automation tools come in. Tools like **Woodpecker, Mailshake,** or **Yesware** can help you set up sequences and track engagement.

- **Schedule follow-ups automatically**: These tools allow you to automate follow-ups based on whether the recipient has opened or replied to your emails.
- **Track engagement**: Use these tools to track open rates, replies, and clicks. This data provides valuable insights to help you refine your strategy.

Conclusion: Timing and Consistency Are Key

The success of your cold email campaign depends on both timing and frequency. By sending emails at optimal times and following up thoughtfully, you increase your chances of reaching prospects when they're most receptive. Remember to space out your follow-ups and add value in every interaction to build relationships without overwhelming your prospects.

Chapter 8: Avoiding Spam Filters

No matter how well-crafted your cold email is, it's useless if it ends up in the spam folder. Email providers like Gmail, Yahoo, and Outlook are constantly updating their algorithms to detect and filter out spam. If you don't take the right steps to ensure your emails are seen as legitimate, you'll struggle to get your messages in front of your prospects. In this chapter, we'll dive into the practical steps you can take to avoid spam filters and maximize your email deliverability.

Understanding How Spam Filters Work

Spam filters are automated systems used by email providers to detect and block unsolicited or unwanted emails. These filters analyze several factors to determine if an email is spam, including the content of the email, your sender reputation, and technical settings like authentication records. Knowing what these filters look for allows you to design your emails and campaigns in ways that help you bypass them.

Set Up Proper Email Authentication

One of the most important steps in avoiding spam filters is setting up proper email authentication. Email providers need to know that your emails are coming from a verified, trustworthy source. Without these technical safeguards, your emails are far more likely to get flagged as spam.

- **SPF (Sender Policy Framework):** SPF tells email servers which domains are authorized to send emails on your behalf. By creating an SPF record in your domain's DNS settings, you provide a list of servers that are allowed to send emails from your domain, making it harder for spammers to forge your domain.

- **DKIM (DomainKeys Identified Mail):** DKIM adds a cryptographic signature to your emails to verify that they were not altered during transmission. This ensures the email's integrity, making it more likely to be trusted by spam filters.

- **DMARC (Domain-based Message Authentication, Reporting, and Conformance):** DMARC ties SPF and DKIM together, giving you control over what happens if an email fails authentication. It also provides reports on your email sending behavior, helping you monitor and improve your email deliverability.

Tip: Use email authentication testing tools like **MXToolbox** or **GlockApps** to ensure that your SPF, DKIM, and DMARC records are correctly set up and functioning.

Maintain a Good Sender Reputation

Your sender reputation is essentially your email trust score. Email providers track how your emails are received and use this data to decide whether to deliver, block, or send your emails to the spam folder. A good sender reputation leads to better deliverability, while a poor one can quickly get your emails blacklisted.

- **Avoid high bounce rates.** Sending emails to invalid or inactive email addresses increases your bounce rate and damages your sender reputation. Before you send an email campaign, use an email verification tool like **NeverBounce** or **ZeroBounce** to clean your list.

- **Monitor spam complaints.** If too many people mark your emails as spam, it sends a signal to email providers that your emails are unwanted. To avoid this, make sure your email offers real value and give recipients an easy way to unsubscribe.

- **Keep a low spam rate.** Your spam rate is the percentage of emails that are flagged as spam by recipients. Aim to keep your spam rate below 0.1% to maintain a positive sender reputation.

Tip: Check your sender reputation regularly using tools like **Sender Score** or **Google Postmaster Tools** to track your email performance and identify any issues.

Avoid Spammy Language and Tactics

Email content plays a big role in determining whether or not your emails get flagged by spam filters. Certain words, phrases, and formatting can trigger spam filters, so it's important to write your emails in a way that appears professional and trustworthy.

- **Avoid spammy words.** Words like "free," "limited time offer," "cash bonus," and "act now" can trigger spam filters. Similarly, overusing punctuation (like exclamation marks) or writing in all caps can cause your email to be flagged.

- **Don't use misleading subject lines.** Your subject line should be clear and relevant to the content of your email. Misleading subject lines, like "Re: Urgent Action Required" or "Important Notice," can not only trigger spam filters but also damage your credibility with the recipient.

- **Minimize excessive formatting.** Avoid using too many colors, large fonts, or overly stylized text in your emails. These tactics can make your email look unprofessional and more likely to be flagged by filters.

Use a Clean Email List

A clean, well-maintained email list is essential for staying out of the spam folder. If you're sending emails to outdated or unverified addresses, you're more likely to see high bounce rates and spam complaints, both of which can damage your deliverability.

- **Remove inactive subscribers.** Regularly clean your list by removing subscribers who haven't engaged with your emails in several months. Continuing to email inactive contacts can hurt your sender reputation.
- **Segment your list.** Not all subscribers are alike, so segment your list based on criteria like industry, job title, or engagement level. Sending targeted emails to specific groups improves relevance and reduces the likelihood of your emails being marked as spam.
- **Avoid buying email lists.** Purchased lists often contain outdated or incorrect email addresses and are more likely to result in high bounce rates or spam complaints. Building your own list through organic methods is always the best approach.

Get Permission Before Sending

Sending cold emails requires a delicate balance, especially in regions with strict data protection regulations. It's essential to ensure that your outreach is compliant with email marketing laws, such as the CAN-SPAM Act, GDPR, and CASL.

- **Include an opt-out option.** Every cold email you send should include a clear and easy way for the recipient to unsubscribe. Failing to provide this option not only violates regulations but also increases the chances of your email being marked as spam.

- **Personalize your outreach.** Personalizing your emails by using the recipient's name, mentioning their company, or referencing something specific to them shows that your email is relevant and not just mass-sent. Personalized emails are less likely to be marked as spam.

- **Use double opt-in for signups.** When collecting email addresses through forms, use a double opt-in process to verify that people actually want to receive your emails. This helps ensure that your list is made up of genuinely interested recipients.

Warm Up Your Domain

If you're starting a cold email campaign from a new domain or haven't sent emails from your domain in a while, it's important to warm up your domain to avoid triggering spam filters. Sending too many emails from a new or inactive domain too quickly can result in low deliverability.

- **Start small.** In the beginning, send emails to a small, targeted group rather than a large batch. Gradually increase the volume over the course of a few weeks to give email providers time to recognize your domain as trustworthy.

- **Engage with your audience.** Focus on sending emails to people who are most likely to open and respond. Positive engagement signals, like high open rates and replies, help build your domain's reputation.

- **Monitor your performance.** Track your open rates, bounce rates, and spam complaints closely during the warm-up period. If you notice any issues, adjust your strategy accordingly before ramping up your campaign.

Test Your Emails Before Sending

Before sending a cold email campaign, it's a good idea to run some tests to make sure your emails won't get caught by spam filters. This can help you spot potential issues and fix them before your campaign goes live.

- **Use spam testing tools.** Tools like **MailGenius**, **Litmus**, and **GlockApps** analyze your email and provide a spam score based on the content, formatting, and technical setup. They'll highlight any issues that could cause your email to be flagged by filters.

- **Check for broken links and images.** Spam filters often flag emails with broken or suspicious links. Make sure that all links work properly and that any images load correctly before sending your campaign.

- **A Warning About Links**: Including too many links or using unfamiliar link shorteners can trigger spam filters. Email providers are wary of emails with excessive links, especially if they point to suspicious or untrusted domains. Stick to one clear call to action with a single, trusted link whenever possible, as this reduces the chance of your email being marked as spam.

- **Review your email on different devices.** Check how your email looks on both desktop and mobile devices to ensure that it displays correctly. Emails that are hard to read or navigate on mobile are more likely to be ignored or deleted, which can hurt engagement rates.

Conclusion: Staying Out of Spam Folders

Avoiding spam filters is essential for the success of your cold email campaigns. By setting up proper email authentication, maintaining a good sender reputation, and sending relevant, personalized emails to clean lists, you significantly increase your chances of landing in the inbox rather than the spam folder. Always test your emails before sending, and be mindful of the language and tactics you use to ensure your messages are both compliant and professional. With these strategies in place, you'll be well on your way to higher open rates, better engagement, and more successful campaigns.

Chapter 9: Automating Cold Emails

Cold emailing is a powerful tool, but manually managing outreach to dozens, hundreds, or even thousands of prospects can be overwhelming and time-consuming. That's where email automation comes in. Automating your cold email campaigns allows you to scale your outreach while keeping your emails timely, relevant, and personalized. In this chapter, we'll explore how to effectively automate your cold email process, the tools you can use, and how to maintain a personal touch even when your emails are automated.

The Benefits of Email Automation

Automation isn't just about saving time. When done right, it can significantly improve the efficiency and effectiveness of your cold email campaigns. Here's why automation can be a game-changer:

- **Scale your outreach**: Instead of sending individual emails to each prospect, you can send personalized emails to large groups at once. This allows you to scale your outreach without sacrificing quality.

- **Follow up without forgetting**: Automated follow-up sequences ensure that no prospect slips through the cracks. You can set up multiple follow-up emails to go out automatically if a prospect doesn't respond, keeping the conversation going without requiring constant manual input.

- **Improve consistency**: When you send emails manually, it's easy for timing and follow-ups to be inconsistent.

Automation ensures that your emails are sent at the right time, every time.

- **Track and optimize**: Most automation tools provide detailed analytics so you can track open rates, click-through rates, and responses in real-time. This data helps you refine your approach and improve future campaigns.

Choosing the Right Automation Tool

There are many tools available for automating cold emails, each offering different features. The right tool for you will depend on your specific needs, but here are some top options:

- **Woodpecker**: Designed for cold email automation, Woodpecker allows you to create personalized campaigns with automated follow-ups. It integrates with popular CRM tools and offers detailed analytics to help optimize your outreach.

- **Mailshake**: A straightforward and effective cold email automation platform. It enables you to send personalized emails, track results, and automate follow-ups. Ideal for sales and marketing teams looking to streamline their outreach.

- **Yesware**: Integrated directly into your email inbox, Yesware offers tracking, template creation, and follow-up automation. It's particularly useful if you want to manage your cold emails without leaving your inbox.

- **Reply.io**: A multi-channel automation tool that covers email and other outreach methods. It includes AI features for lead generation, personalized email sequences, and detailed analytics.

- **Apollo.io**: Combining cold email automation with lead generation, Apollo.io is a great choice if you want a tool that helps automate emails while also finding new leads.

Pro Tip: When choosing a tool, look for features that allow for easy personalization, A/B testing, and integration with your existing CRM. These capabilities will help you streamline your workflow and improve your results.

Setting Up Automated Cold Email Sequences

A cold email sequence is a series of automated emails sent over time. The goal is to engage prospects who didn't respond to your initial message by gradually adding more value and urgency. A well-crafted sequence ensures you stay top of mind without being too aggressive.

Here's how to set up an effective automated email sequence:

- Start with your initial email: This is where you introduce yourself, explain the value you offer, and prompt the recipient to take action (e.g., schedule a call or reply to your email). Make sure this email is personalized and focused on the recipient's needs.

- Schedule your first follow-up: If the recipient doesn't respond, send a follow-up a few days later (typically 3-5 days). In this email, reference your first message and add more value—perhaps by sharing a relevant case study or highlighting a specific solution you provide.

- Send a second follow-up: If there's still no response, send another follow-up after about a week. This email should offer new insights, ask a different question, or provide another valuable resource.

- Final follow-up: After three or four emails, send a final follow-up. This message should be polite and non-pushy, leaving the door open for future communication. For example, "I understand now might not be the right time. If you're ever interested in discussing [offer], feel free to reach out."

Example of an automated sequence:

- **Initial Email:** Introduce yourself, explain your offer, and prompt the recipient to take action.

- **First Follow-up (Day 3-5):** "Just following up" email that references your initial message and adds more value.

- **Second Follow-up (Day 7-10):** Continue to add value, offer a resource, or ask a different question.

- **Final Follow-up (Day 14-20):** Send a polite, final message and leave the door open for future contact.

Personalization in Automated Emails

One of the common concerns with automation is that it can feel impersonal. Fortunately, most email automation tools allow you to personalize at scale, ensuring that each email feels relevant and unique to the recipient.

Here's how to personalize your automated emails:

- Use merge tags: Most automation tools allow you to insert personalized fields like the recipient's first name, company name, or job title. This makes your emails feel more customized and relevant.

- Reference specific details: If you've researched the prospect, mention something specific about their business or industry. Even one personalized sentence can significantly increase engagement.

- Segment your list: Rather than sending the same email to everyone, segment your list based on criteria like job role, company size, or industry. This allows you to tailor your message to each group.

Example of personalization:

Hi [First Name],

I noticed that [Company] has been expanding in [specific industry/market], and I thought you might find our [product/service] useful for reaching new customers. We've helped similar companies like [Client Name] increase their conversions by 20% in just a few months.

Testing and Optimizing Your Sequences

Automation isn't a "set it and forget it" solution. You'll need to continuously test and optimize your email sequences to maximize their effectiveness. Here's how to do it:

- **A/B test subject lines**: Test different subject lines to see which ones yield the highest open rates. For example, try variations such as personal vs. professional tone or questions vs. statements.

- **Experiment with timing**: Test sending follow-up emails at different intervals to determine when your prospects are most likely to respond. For example, compare 3-day vs. 7-day follow-ups.

- **Monitor performance metrics**: Track open rates, click-through rates, and response rates. If open rates are low, focus on improving your subject lines. If response rates are low, tweak the content of your emails.

- **Refine your CTA**: If you're not getting the desired responses, test different calls to action. Asking for smaller commitments, like a quick call or simple reply, can sometimes yield better results than pushing for a larger ask upfront.

Automating Multi-Channel Outreach

While email is a powerful tool, automating your outreach doesn't have to be limited to emails. Many tools now support multi-channel outreach, allowing you to engage prospects via platforms like LinkedIn or phone calls.

- **LinkedIn automation**: Tools like Expandi or Dux-Soup let you automate LinkedIn connection requests and follow-up messages. Combining LinkedIn with your email outreach increases your visibility, especially for recipients more active on social media.

- **Phone call automation**: Some platforms include features to schedule automated reminders for follow-up calls, ensuring you don't miss an opportunity to connect.

- **Social media outreach**: Automating outreach through social platforms like Twitter or Facebook can help you stay on your prospect's radar, increasing the likelihood of engagement.

Conclusion: Streamline Without Losing the Personal Touch

Automating your cold emails is a smart way to scale your outreach, save time, and ensure consistency. However, it's important to balance automation with personalization to keep your emails engaging and relevant. By using the right tools, setting up thoughtful sequences, and continuously testing your approach, you can reach more prospects while maintaining the personal touch that makes cold emailing effective. The goal of automation isn't to replace human interaction—it's to enhance it, allowing you to focus on building relationships while automating repetitive tasks.

Chapter 10: Case Studies and Success Stories

There's no better way to learn about the effectiveness of cold emailing than by looking at real-world examples. Case studies and success stories provide tangible proof that cold emailing works when done correctly. In this chapter, I'll share some examples of businesses and professionals who've used cold email outreach to generate leads, close deals, and grow their businesses. These stories not only illustrate successful tactics but also highlight the importance of persistence, personalization, and strategic planning.

Case Study 1: A SaaS Company Grows Its Client Base by 30% with Cold Emails

The Challenge:
A small SaaS company specializing in project management tools was struggling to break into new markets. Despite having a solid product, their marketing efforts were falling short. They were relying heavily on inbound marketing and referrals but needed a more direct way to reach decision-makers at medium to large businesses.

The Strategy:
The company decided to launch a cold email campaign targeting project managers and operations directors at medium-sized tech firms. They began by identifying their ideal prospects through LinkedIn and other lead generation tools. Each cold email was highly personalized and addressed specific pain points the prospects were likely facing, such as team coordination issues and missed deadlines.

Their email sequence included:

1. An introductory email that mentioned their product's ability to streamline team collaboration and reduce project delays.

2. A follow-up email three days later with a case study of a similar company that saw a 20% increase in project completion rates after implementing their tool.

3. A final follow-up a week later that included a free trial offer and a personal note from the CEO inviting them to discuss their needs.

The Results:
The company saw a 30% increase in its client base within three months. The cold emails achieved a 35% open rate and a 10% response rate. The personalized, value-driven approach resonated with prospects, leading to 15 new clients and significantly boosting their revenue.

Takeaway:
Personalization and targeting are key. By addressing specific pain points and offering a clear, actionable value proposition, the SaaS company was able to stand out in a crowded market. The free trial offer in the final follow-up also lowered the barrier to entry, encouraging more prospects to take action.

Case Study 2: A Marketing Agency Lands High-Profile Clients with Cold Emailing

The Challenge:
A boutique digital marketing agency wanted to land bigger clients in the eCommerce industry but lacked the connections to get their foot in the door. They needed a way to reach decision-makers at larger eCommerce brands and demonstrate their expertise in driving online sales.

The Strategy:
The agency created a cold email campaign targeting eCommerce brands that were struggling with cart abandonment. They crafted a series of three emails, each one focusing on a different aspect of how they could help reduce cart abandonment and increase conversions.

The email sequence looked like this:

1. The first email introduced the agency, explained their specialization in eCommerce marketing, and shared a relevant statistic: "Did you know that nearly 70% of online shopping carts are abandoned before purchase? We've helped brands like [Brand Name] reduce that number by 15%."

2. The second email offered a case study from a previous client who saw a significant improvement in sales after implementing the agency's strategies.

3. The final email included a limited-time offer for a free consultation, aimed at showing them how they could improve their own cart abandonment rates.

The Results:
Within six weeks, the agency landed two high-profile clients, including a fast-growing eCommerce brand. The cold emails achieved a 40% open rate, and one client even replied within just hours of receiving the first email. The focus on a specific problem (cart abandonment) that the agency could solve was key to their success.

Takeaway:
Focusing on a single pain point and offering a solution backed by case studies helped the agency demonstrate their expertise and value. This approach, combined with a clear call to action (a free consultation), gave prospects a reason to engage with the emails.

Case Study 3: A Consultant Generates $100,000 in Revenue from Cold Emailing

The Challenge:
A freelance business consultant specializing in helping small businesses scale was struggling to attract new clients. Traditional networking and word-of-mouth referrals weren't bringing in enough leads, so they decided to try cold emailing as a more proactive approach.

The Strategy:
The consultant targeted small business owners in the technology and service industries who were likely facing growth challenges. They used email automation to send personalized cold emails at scale, with a focus on offering a free "business growth audit" to identify areas for improvement.

The email sequence included:

1. An introductory email explaining how the audit could uncover hidden opportunities for growth and offering a free consultation.

2. A follow-up email five days later providing a short case study of a similar client who had doubled their revenue after working with the consultant.

3. A final email that reiterated the offer and added a sense of urgency: "This offer is available to just a few businesses this month, so let me know if you'd like to reserve a spot."

The Results:
Within six months, the consultant had signed several new clients, generating over $100,000 in revenue. The cold emails had an open rate of 30% and a response rate of 8%. Many of the prospects who

responded were business owners who hadn't actively been looking for consulting services but were intrigued by the audit offer.

Takeaway:
Offering something of value upfront, like a free audit, can be a powerful way to engage prospects and build trust. The consultant's willingness to offer advice before asking for anything in return helped establish credibility and open the door to new business opportunities.

Case Study 4: A B2B Sales Team Closes $250,000 in New Deals with Cold Emails

The Challenge:
A B2B sales team for a software company was struggling to book meetings with potential clients. They had a solid product but found that decision-makers were often too busy to respond to their outreach efforts. They needed a way to cut through the noise and grab the attention of IT managers at large companies.

The Strategy:
The team launched a cold email campaign that focused on solving a specific problem for IT departments: managing multiple software licenses across different platforms. Their emails were short, to the point, and addressed the exact pain points IT managers often faced.

The email sequence was as follows:

1. The first email highlighted the problem of software license management and introduced their tool as a solution.
2. The second email included a link to a short video demo of their software in action, showing how it could simplify the license management process.

3. The final follow-up email offered a limited-time discount for companies that signed up for a free demo within the next two weeks.

The Results:
The campaign resulted in over $250,000 in new business, with an open rate of 45% and a 15% response rate. IT managers appreciated the concise, problem-solving nature of the emails, and the video demo helped them visualize how the software could fit into their existing systems.

Takeaway:
When targeting busy decision-makers, keeping your emails short and focused on solving a specific problem can lead to high engagement. The use of a video demo added a visual element that made it easier for prospects to see the value of the product without committing to a sales call.

Lessons from Success Stories

These case studies highlight several important lessons for anyone looking to succeed with cold emailing:

- **Personalization works.** Whether you're targeting CEOs or IT managers, personalized emails that reference the recipient's specific needs and pain points consistently perform better than generic mass emails.

- **Follow-up is crucial.** Many of these success stories involved multiple follow-up emails. Sending one email is rarely enough. A well-timed follow-up can reignite interest and bring your email back to the top of the recipient's inbox.

- **Offer value upfront.** Free trials, consultations, and audits can be highly effective in getting prospects to engage with your emails. By offering something of value before asking for a sale, you build trust and create an incentive for the recipient to take action.

- **Solve a problem.** The best cold emails focus on solving a specific problem for the recipient. Whether it's increasing sales, reducing costs, or saving time, showing how you can provide a solution gives the recipient a reason to respond.

Conclusion: Inspiration for Your Campaigns

These case studies are proof that cold emailing, when done right, can yield impressive results. By focusing on personalization, targeting specific pain points, and offering something of value, you can replicate these successes in your own campaigns. As you plan your cold email strategy, remember the key elements that made these campaigns work: persistence, value, and problem-solving. Use these stories as inspiration and a guide for how to craft your next winning campaign.

Chapter 11: Measuring Success

You've sent your cold emails, set up follow-up sequences, and waited for responses. But how do you know if your campaign is working? Measuring success is about more than just counting replies—it's about understanding how each part of your cold email process contributes to your goals. In this chapter, we'll dive into the metrics you should track, how to interpret the results, and what actions to take to improve your campaigns moving forward.

Key Metrics to Track

Before you can measure success, you need to know which metrics matter most in a cold email campaign. These metrics provide insight into what's working and what needs adjustment.

1. **Open Rate**
   The open rate tells you how many of your recipients opened your email. This metric is important because it shows how effective your subject line and sender name are at grabbing attention. If your open rate is low, it might mean that your subject lines aren't compelling enough or that your emails are getting caught in spam filters.

   Benchmark:
   A good open rate for cold emails typically falls between 35% and 40%, although certain campaigns can see open rates as high as 80% with proper split testing and optimization.

   How to Improve:
   - Test different subject lines. A/B test subject lines to see which ones lead to higher open rates.

- Use personalization. Including the recipient's name or company name in the subject line can increase open rates.
- Ensure your emails aren't going to spam. Set up proper email authentication (SPF, DKIM, DMARC) to improve deliverability.

2. **Response Rate**

The response rate measures the percentage of people who replied to your email. It's one of the most important metrics for determining the overall effectiveness of your campaign. A high response rate means your email content is resonating with your audience, while a low response rate suggests you may need to refine your message or target audience.

Benchmark:
A typical cold email response rate ranges from 20% to 60%, depending on the niche and the quality of the personalization in the email campaign.

How to Improve:

- Personalize your emails. Highly personalized emails tend to get better responses. Mention the recipient's company, job role, or recent accomplishments.
- Clarify your call to action. Make sure your emails have a clear, simple call to action (CTA), such as scheduling a call or replying with a yes/no answer.
- Follow up. Sending two or three follow-up emails can significantly boost response rates.

3. **Click-Through Rate (CTR)**

If your cold email includes a link—such as to a case study, landing page, or demo video—the click-through rate tells you how many people clicked on that link. CTR helps you understand how well your content is engaging recipients and driving them to take action.

Benchmark:

A typical CTR for cold emails is between 2% and 10%, though this can vary based on the type of link you include.

How to Improve:

- Make your links relevant. Only include links that provide clear value, such as a case study that solves a problem they face or a product demo relevant to their needs.

- Test different CTAs. Try using different wording for your call to action, such as "Learn more" or "See how it works."

- Reduce distractions. Keep the email focused on one action—too many links or calls to action can confuse the recipient and reduce clicks.

4. **Conversion Rate**

    The conversion rate is the percentage of recipients who completed the desired action, such as booking a meeting, signing up for a free trial, or making a purchase. This is the ultimate measure of success in a cold email campaign, as it shows how many of your prospects turned into leads or customers.

    Benchmark:

    Conversion rates vary widely by industry and niche. For instance:

    - Highly competitive niches like chiropractors or dentists can expect around 1%.

- Niche markets, such as flight schools, can achieve conversion rates of 11% or more.

- Some markets like restaurant equipment or specialized service providers can see conversion rates as high as 9% to 12%.

How to Improve:

- Offer clear value. Make sure your offer (whether it's a free trial, consultation, or demo) is attractive and clearly communicated in the email.

- Build trust. Including case studies, testimonials, or social proof in your emails can increase conversion rates by building credibility with your audience.

- Use scarcity and urgency. Phrases like "limited spots available" or "offer ends soon" can encourage recipients to act quickly.

5. **Bounce Rate**
The bounce rate refers to the percentage of emails that couldn't be delivered to recipients. There are two types of bounces: hard bounces and soft bounces. Hard bounces occur when an email address is invalid, while soft bounces happen due to temporary issues like a full inbox or server problem.

Benchmark:
Aim for a bounce rate of less than 2%. Anything higher could indicate problems with your email list quality.

How to Improve:

- Clean your email list regularly. Use email verification tools like **NeverBounce** or **ZeroBounce** to ensure you're sending emails to valid addresses.

- Monitor your bounce rate. If you notice a high bounce rate, pause your campaign and clean your list before resuming.

Analyzing and Interpreting the Data

Once you've tracked the key metrics, the next step is to analyze the data to understand how your campaign is performing. Here's a step-by-step process for evaluating your cold email campaign:

1. **Identify patterns.** Look for trends in your open rates, response rates, and CTRs across different emails in your sequence. Are some subject lines performing better than others? Is your response rate improving with follow-up emails?

2. **Segment your results.** Break down your metrics by audience segments, such as job titles, industries, or company sizes. You may find that certain segments respond better to specific messaging or offers.

3. **Compare against benchmarks.** Use the industry benchmarks provided earlier to gauge your campaign's performance. If your open rates are below the benchmark, focus on improving your subject lines or email deliverability. If your response rate is low, consider revising your email content.

4. **Identify weak points.** If your campaign isn't meeting expectations, look for specific areas to improve. For example, if your open rates are high but your response rates are low, the problem may lie in your email body or CTA.

5. **Evaluate your overall success.** Look beyond individual metrics to assess your overall campaign performance. Did

you achieve your primary goal, whether that was booking meetings, generating leads, or driving sales?

A/B Testing for Continuous Improvement

One of the best ways to optimize your cold email campaigns is through A/B testing. A/B testing involves sending two different versions of an email to different segments of your audience to see which version performs better. By testing different elements, you can refine your approach and gradually improve your results.

Here's what you can A/B test:

- **Subject lines:** Try testing a personalized subject line vs. a more general one. For example, "Increase [Company Name]'s efficiency by 30%" vs. "New tool to boost productivity."

- **Email copy:** Experiment with different tones or lengths of your email. Does a more conversational approach work better than a formal one? Does a shorter email get more responses than a longer one?

- **Calls to action:** Test different CTAs to see what drives more clicks or responses. For example, "Schedule a call" vs. "Reply to this email with your availability."

- **Timing:** Test sending your emails at different times of day or on different days of the week to see when your audience is most responsive.

Making Data-Driven Decisions

The ultimate goal of tracking and analyzing metrics is to make data-driven decisions that improve the effectiveness of your cold email campaigns. Here are a few steps you can take to act on your findings:

- **Optimize your next campaign.** Use the insights from your current campaign to make adjustments for your next one. If you noticed certain segments responded better to a specific message, tailor future campaigns accordingly.

- **Adjust your follow-up strategy.** If you see that responses tend to come after the second or third follow-up, consider adjusting the frequency or content of your follow-up emails for better results.

- **Refine your targeting.** If certain audience segments aren't responding well, refine your targeting criteria to focus on prospects who are more likely to engage with your emails.

Tracking Long-Term Performance

Cold emailing isn't just about short-term results. To get the most out of your campaigns, you need to track performance over the long term. This includes looking at metrics like:

- **Lifetime value of new clients.** If your cold email campaigns lead to new customers, track the long-term value of those relationships. How much revenue do these clients generate over time?

- **Lead nurturing.** Even if a cold email doesn't lead to an immediate conversion, it can still help build a relationship with the prospect. Track how many cold email recipients eventually convert after engaging with your content over time.

Conclusion: Measure, Optimize, and Repeat

Measuring the success of your cold email campaigns is essential to improving your results and achieving your goals. By tracking key metrics like open rates, response rates, and conversion rates, you can identify what's working and what needs improvement. Use A/B testing to continuously refine your approach, and make data-driven decisions to optimize your campaigns for maximum impact. Remember, cold emailing is a process of constant learning and adaptation, and by consistently measuring and improving, you'll see better results over time.

Chapter 12: Scaling Your Cold Email Outreach

Once you've nailed down a cold email strategy that works, the next step is scaling your outreach. Scaling doesn't just mean sending more emails — it means increasing your volume while maintaining the quality and personalization that make your emails effective in the first place. In this chapter, we'll look at how to expand your cold email efforts without sacrificing relevance, how to manage larger campaigns efficiently, and the tools you can use to streamline the process.

Why Scaling Matters

Scaling your cold email outreach allows you to reach more prospects, generate more leads, and close more deals. However, there's a risk that as you increase volume, your emails could become less personal and less targeted. A well-scaled campaign balances efficiency with personalization to ensure you continue building meaningful relationships with prospects.

- **Reach more people, without losing the personal touch.** A major challenge when scaling is making sure your emails still feel personalized. Scaling effectively means continuing to treat your prospects like individuals, not just entries in a mass email list.

- **Improve lead generation.** With a higher volume of emails, you can reach more prospects in less time. Scaling allows you to test different audiences and segments, identifying untapped markets and new opportunities.

- **Enhance efficiency.** Scaling helps you maximize the return on your efforts by optimizing your workflow and processes.

With the right tools and strategies, you can increase your outreach while reducing manual work.

Preparing to Scale: Start with a Solid Foundation

Before you start scaling your cold email outreach, you need to have a solid foundation in place. If your email process isn't optimized or you're still testing different approaches, it's best to refine these elements first before ramping up your efforts. Scaling a campaign that isn't working will only amplify the problems.

- **Refine your strategy.** Make sure you've nailed down your email copy, subject lines, and follow-up sequences. If you haven't achieved solid response rates and conversions at a smaller scale, focus on optimizing these factors before scaling.
- **Optimize your workflow.** As you scale, efficiency becomes more important. Ensure that your tools, processes, and workflows are in place so that you can manage a larger volume of emails without running into bottlenecks.
- **Clean your email list.** Before scaling, make sure your email list is up to date and free of inactive or unverified addresses. A clean list will reduce bounce rates and improve deliverability as you ramp up your outreach.

Segmenting Your Audience for Effective Scaling

Segmenting your audience is one of the most important steps in scaling your cold email outreach. By breaking your list into targeted segments, you can tailor your messaging to different groups, making your emails more relevant and increasing the chances of a response.

- **Segment by job role.** Different decision-makers in a company (such as CEOs, marketing managers, and IT directors) have different priorities. Tailor your emails to each role by addressing their specific pain points and how your solution can help them.

- **Segment by industry.** Industries have unique challenges, and your emails should reflect that. For example, an email targeting healthcare companies might focus on regulatory compliance, while one aimed at tech startups might emphasize scalability and speed.

- **Segment by company size.** The size of a company can influence its needs and budget. Larger companies may need more complex, enterprise-level solutions, while smaller businesses are often looking for affordability and ease of use. Your email should reflect these differences.

Automating at Scale

When scaling your cold email outreach, automation becomes essential. Tools like **Mailshake**, **Woodpecker**, and **Reply.io** can help you automate your email sequences, follow-ups, and personalization, allowing you to reach hundreds or thousands of prospects without manual effort.

- **Set up automated sequences.** With automation tools, you can create email sequences that automatically send follow-ups based on whether the recipient opened or replied to your previous emails. This ensures that no prospect slips through the cracks and that your follow-up process remains consistent.

- **Use merge tags for personalization.** Automation tools allow you to insert personalized fields (such as the recipient's name, company, or industry) into your emails. This lets you scale without losing the personal touch that's essential for effective cold emailing.

- **Monitor your campaigns in real-time.** Automation platforms provide detailed analytics, such as open rates, response rates, and click-through rates. This data allows you to track the performance of your emails and adjust your approach as needed.

Balancing Personalization with Volume

As you scale, maintaining personalization can become challenging. Sending out hundreds or thousands of emails makes it harder to craft unique messages for each prospect. However, there are strategies you can use to personalize emails at scale without sacrificing quality.

- **Create email templates for different segments.** Instead of writing each email from scratch, create a set of templates tailored to different audience segments. Each template should address the specific needs and pain points of that segment. You can then personalize the opening line or closing statement for each recipient.

- **Personalize key details.** Even when scaling, small touches of personalization can make a big difference. Use automation to insert the recipient's name, company name, or a specific detail about their business (like a recent achievement or challenge) into the email. This makes the email feel more relevant to the recipient.

- **Leverage dynamic content.** Some email automation tools allow you to insert dynamic content based on the recipient's data. For example, you can customize the subject line, body text, or CTA based on the recipient's role, industry, or location.

Managing Larger Campaigns Efficiently

Scaling your cold email outreach requires efficient management, especially when dealing with large volumes of prospects. Without the right tools and processes in place, managing a scaled campaign can become overwhelming. Here are some strategies to manage your campaigns efficiently:

- **Use a CRM for lead tracking.** As your outreach expands, it's important to track interactions with each prospect. A CRM system like **HubSpot**, **Pipedrive**, or **Salesforce** can help you organize your leads, track email engagement, and manage follow-ups. Integrating your CRM with your email automation tool allows for seamless management of your campaigns.

- **Automate follow-up reminders.** Automation tools can also remind you to follow up manually with high-priority prospects. For example, if a key decision-maker has opened your email several times but hasn't responded, you can be alerted to follow up personally.

- **Outsource list-building or research.** Building and cleaning email lists at scale can be time-consuming. Consider outsourcing list-building or lead research to specialized services or virtual assistants to free up your time for higher-level strategy.

Testing and Optimizing at Scale

When scaling your cold email outreach, continuous testing and optimization become even more critical. As your volume increases, small improvements in open rates or response rates can have a significant impact on overall performance.

- **A/B test subject lines.** Test different subject lines across your campaigns to see which ones drive higher open rates. For example, try personal vs. general subject lines, or test different tones (formal vs. casual).
- **Test email copy.** Experiment with different email lengths, formats, and CTAs. Does a short, direct email perform better than a more detailed one? Does asking a question in the first line increase response rates? Test these variables to find what works best.
- **Track performance by segment.** Analyze the performance of your campaigns by segment (such as industry or job role). You may find that certain segments respond better to specific messaging, which can help you further refine your emails.

Scaling While Maintaining Deliverability

One of the risks of scaling cold email outreach is damaging your email deliverability. Sending a high volume of emails too quickly can trigger spam filters, resulting in poor inbox placement and lower response rates. Here's how to scale without compromising deliverability:

- **Warm up your email domain.** If you're ramping up email volume, do it gradually. Start by sending a small number of emails per day and slowly increase the volume over time. This gives email providers a chance to recognize your domain as trustworthy.

- **Use multiple email addresses.** To reduce the risk of your emails being marked as spam, consider using multiple email addresses from the same domain. This spreads out your volume and reduces the chances of triggering spam filters.

- **Monitor your sender reputation.** Use tools like **Google Postmaster Tools** or **Sender Score** to track your sender reputation and ensure your emails are landing in inboxes, not spam folders.

Conclusion: Scale Smart, Not Just Fast

Scaling your cold email outreach can unlock significant growth for your business, but it requires careful planning and execution. By segmenting your audience, automating effectively, and maintaining personalization, you can increase your volume without sacrificing the quality of your emails. Testing and optimization are key to ensuring that your campaigns continue to perform well at scale. Most importantly, always prioritize deliverability and relevance, ensuring that your emails reach the right people at the right time.

Chapter 13: Common Mistakes and How to Avoid Them

Cold emailing can be highly effective, but it's easy to make mistakes that derail your efforts. From weak subject lines to targeting the wrong audience, even small missteps can lead to low response rates, poor deliverability, and wasted time. In this chapter, we'll explore common mistakes people make in cold email campaigns and offer actionable tips on how to avoid them.

1. Targeting the Wrong Audience

One of the most common mistakes in cold emailing is sending your message to people who aren't the right fit. Even the best-written email won't get a response if it lands in the wrong inbox.

- **The Problem:**
  A major issue in cold emailing is sending your message to people who aren't the right fit. No matter how well-crafted your email is, if it lands in the wrong inbox, it's likely to be ignored.

- **The Fix:**
  Focus on quality over quantity. Narrow your audience by considering factors like industry, job title, company size, and specific pain points. Use tools such as LinkedIn Sales Navigator or industry databases to find decision-makers who are more likely to be interested in your product or service.

2. Sending Generic, Impersonal Emails

Another common mistake is sending generic, one-size-fits-all emails that don't feel personal. People can tell when they're receiving a mass email, and it often leads to immediate deletion.

- **The Problem:**
  Generic, one-size-fits-all emails are easy to spot and often dismissed. People can tell when they've received a mass email that lacks personal relevance.

- **The Fix:**
  Personalize each email. Use the recipient's name, mention their company, and reference something specific about their business or industry. Even small personal touches, like recognizing a recent achievement, can make a big difference. Automation tools with merge tags allow you to personalize emails at scale while keeping them relevant.

3. Writing Weak Subject Lines

The subject line is the first thing your recipient sees, and it plays a critical role in whether or not your email gets opened. A weak or unclear subject line can ruin even the best email.

- **The Problem:**
  Subject lines are your first impression, and a weak or vague subject line can prevent your email from being opened. If it's too salesy or unclear, it can lower your open rates.

- **The Fix:**
  Craft short, compelling subject lines that grab attention. Keep them under 50 characters and make sure they highlight a benefit or spark curiosity. Avoid using spammy words like "free" or "urgent." You can also A/B test subject lines to determine which resonate best with your audience.

  Examples of strong subject lines:
    - "Quick idea to increase [Company Name]'s lead generation"
    - "Can we help you solve [specific problem]?"

- "How [Company X] boosted conversions by 20% in 3 months"

4. Ignoring Email Deliverability

Your emails may never reach the inbox if you're not paying attention to deliverability. Many cold email campaigns fail simply because emails end up in spam folders or are blocked entirely.

- **The Problem:**
  If your emails aren't landing in the recipient's inbox, you won't get responses. Poor deliverability often occurs due to improper email setup or over-aggressive sending practices.

- **The Fix:**
  Ensure proper email authentication by setting up SPF, DKIM, and DMARC records for your domain. Regularly clean your email list to remove inactive or invalid addresses, and gradually warm up your domain if sending large volumes. Avoid spammy language to maintain your sender reputation and reduce the chance of your emails being flagged as spam.

5. Neglecting Follow-Up Emails

Many cold email campaigns fail because people stop after the first email. In most cases, one email isn't enough to get a response — follow-up emails are essential.

- **The Problem:**
  One of the biggest mistakes is failing to follow up after the initial email. Most prospects won't respond to the first email, and without a follow-up, you're missing an opportunity.

- **The Fix:**
  Plan a sequence of 2-3 follow-up emails, spaced a few days to a week apart. Each follow-up should add value rather than just asking if they saw your previous email. You can

offer additional information, such as a case study or a resource, to keep the conversation going.

6. Overcomplicating Your Emails

A cold email that's too long or filled with unnecessary details will lose the recipient's interest quickly. Simplicity and clarity are key.

- **The Problem:**
  Long, dense emails filled with too much information often overwhelm recipients and obscure your main point, leading them to ignore or delete the email.

- **The Fix:**
  Keep your emails short and focused. Introduce yourself, explain your value proposition clearly, and include a simple call to action (CTA), like scheduling a brief call. If they want more information, they'll ask for it. Simplicity leads to higher engagement.

7. Asking for Too Much, Too Soon

Cold emails should be focused on starting a conversation, not closing a deal. Asking for too much, like a big commitment or sale in the first email, can turn prospects off.

- **The Problem:**
  Some cold emails push too hard for a sale or a large commitment upfront, which can overwhelm or turn off prospects.

- **The Fix:**
  Start small. Rather than asking for a big commitment, like a long demo or sales meeting, request a brief 10-15 minute conversation. Your goal should be to open a dialogue, not to close a deal in the first interaction.

8. Failing to Provide Value

If your email doesn't offer clear value to the recipient, they're unlikely to respond. Cold emails that are all about you and your product, rather than the recipient's needs, won't resonate.

- **The Problem:**
  Many cold emails focus too much on the sender and what they're selling, without addressing the recipient's needs or pain points. This makes the email feel irrelevant.

- **The Fix:**
  Shift the focus from selling to solving. Clearly explain how your product or service can help the recipient solve a problem or achieve a goal. Highlight the specific value you bring to the table and why it's relevant to them. The more you focus on their needs, the more likely they are to respond.

9. Sending Emails at the Wrong Time

Even the best cold email can fail if it's sent at the wrong time. Timing matters, and sending emails at the right time can significantly improve open and response rates.

- **The Problem:**
  Even a well-crafted email can fail if it's sent at an inopportune time, such as during the weekend or late at night. Timing has a significant impact on whether your email gets noticed.

- **The Fix:**
  Send emails during business hours, ideally on Tuesday, Wednesday, or Thursday mornings. Avoid sending emails on weekends or late in the evening unless you know your audience's habits. Use scheduling tools to ensure your emails are delivered at the optimal time for your recipient's time zone.

Conclusion: Learning from Mistakes

Cold emailing can be incredibly effective, but only if you avoid common mistakes. By targeting the right audience, personalizing your emails, refining your subject lines, and paying attention to timing and deliverability, you'll increase your chances of success. Remember that cold emailing is a process of continuous learning and improvement. By avoiding these common pitfalls and optimizing your approach, you'll be well-positioned to see long-term results from your campaigns.

Bonus 1: Cold Email Subject Line Cheat Sheet

1. **Curiosity-Driven Subject Lines**
    - "Are you optimizing your conversion rate?"
    - "Can we help improve [company]'s lead generation?"
    - "Struggling to turn visitors into customers?"

2. **Value-Focused Subject Lines**
    - "Quick tip to increase conversions for [company]"
    - "Helping [company] reduce churn by 20%"
    - "How [similar company] boosted sales by 30%"

3. **Problem-Solving Subject Lines**
    - "Struggling with [specific pain point]? Here's a solution."
    - "Tired of missing out on leads? Let's fix that."
    - "Overcoming [specific challenge] with this simple method"

4. **Case Study-Based Subject Lines**
    - "How [company] improved [metric] by 30% in 3 months"
    - "How [similar company] boosted sales by 30%"
    - "Helping [company] increase leads by 20% — learn how"

5. **Urgency-Based Subject Lines**
    - "Limited time: Unlock 20% more leads in [specific time]"

- "Only a few spots left for a free consultation this month"
- "Don't miss out on improving [specific goal] — here's how"

6. **Personalized Subject Lines**
   - "Hi [First Name], can I help [Company] reduce churn?"
   - "[First Name], here's a quick tip to increase [specific business area]"
   - "Helping [Company] improve [specific goal] — interested?"

This cheat sheet gives you a diverse set of subject lines that align with both curiosity and value-driven approaches, while maintaining personalization and relevance. Each subject line is crafted to grab attention, highlight benefits, and maintain consistency with cold email best practices.

Bonus 2: Overcoming Common Cold Email Objections

When cold emailing, it's common to face objections—whether they're explicit or implied in a lack of response. Knowing how to handle objections will improve your chances of converting a cold prospect into a warm lead. Here's how to overcome the most common objections you might encounter in cold email outreach.

1. "We're not interested right now."

Response Strategy:
Acknowledge their position without being pushy, but leave the door open for future contact. You can also probe to understand the specific reason for their lack of interest.

Example Reply:
"Thanks for letting me know! I completely understand—timing is everything. Out of curiosity, is there a specific challenge you're focusing on right now? I'd love to stay in touch in case we can assist when the time is right."

2. "We already have a provider."

Response Strategy:
This objection can be an opportunity to differentiate yourself from their current provider. Focus on how you offer a unique value or a better solution.

Example Reply:
"That's great to hear! Many of our current clients were also satisfied with their providers before they made the switch to us. I'd be happy to show you a quick comparison on how we helped companies like yours reduce costs by 20% without changing their existing workflow. Would you be open to a quick call?"

3. "I don't have time for this."

Response Strategy:
Respect their time and offer a quick, no-commitment option. Emphasize the brevity of your meeting or the immediate value they will gain.

Example Reply:
"I totally understand — you're busy! That's exactly why I suggest a quick 10-minute chat, just to see if this could save you time in the long run. If now isn't ideal, is there a better time that works for you?"

4. "We don't have the budget."

Response Strategy:
Show understanding of their financial concerns and offer a solution that may fit their budget or highlight how your product can provide ROI.

Example Reply:
"I understand budgets are tight. That's why I wanted to discuss how we've helped companies in your industry reduce operational costs. Would you be open to a brief chat to see if this could be a cost-saving solution for you?"

5. "We're too small/big for this."

Response Strategy:
Tailor your response to show how your solution is scalable, whether they're a small startup or a large organization. Offer examples of clients similar in size.

Example Reply:
"I hear you! We work with companies of all sizes, and I've found that businesses like [Client Name] have seen great results with our approach, no matter their scale. Could we schedule a quick call to explore how we might help [Company]?"

6. "Send me more information."

Response Strategy:
This is a softer objection but can often lead to nothing if not handled correctly. Instead of sending a generic brochure, suggest a more interactive approach, like a call or demo.

Example Reply:
"I'd be happy to send over some details, but I've found that a quick 10-minute chat is the best way to determine exactly what's most relevant to your needs. Would you have some time later this week?"

7. "This isn't a priority right now."

Response Strategy:
Position your solution as something that could alleviate a current challenge or prevent future issues, showing them why it's worth considering sooner rather than later.

Example Reply:
"I completely understand, and priorities shift quickly. However, I thought this might help [Company] tackle [specific challenge] without requiring much effort on your part. Could we have a quick chat to see if this could support your current objectives?"

Bonus Resource: Cold Email Wizard

Get help crafting high-converting cold emails instantly!

Just scan the QR code below to access the **Cold Email Wizard**, designed to help you write effective cold emails based on the strategies in this book.

How it works:

1. **Scan the QR Code**.
2. **Sign up for a free OpenAI account** (if you don't already have one).
3. **Ask the Cold Email Wizard** for help with your email.

That's it! Whether you need subject lines, email templates, or follow-up sequences, the Wizard is here to help.

Scan to Access:

This resource will get you started fast with cold emails that convert!

A Few Last Words

You now have the strategies and tools to master cold emailing, but success comes from action, not just knowledge. Start small, refine your approach, and stay consistent. Cold emailing is about building relationships and offering value, not just sending messages.

Track your results, adapt as needed, and keep learning. Digital marketing evolves, and so should your strategy. With the insights from this book, you're ready to generate leads, open doors, and build connections. Now, it's time to take action and see the results.

Here's to your success!

/Stefan Florin

www.ingramcontent.com/pod-product-compliance
Lightning Source LLC
Chambersburg PA
CBHW070348230526
45471CB00006B/2473